The Zen Parent Guide
Raising Kids with a Smile

Amy Giustino Talbot

• CHICAGO •

The Zen Parent Guide
Raising Kids with a Smile
Amy Giustino Talbot

JoshuaTreePublishing.com
• Chicago •

All rights reserved. No part of this book may be reproduced or transmitted in any form or by any means, electronic or mechanical, including information storage and retrieval system without written permission from the publisher, except by a reviewer who may quote brief passages in a review.

ISBN 13-Digit: 978-1-941049-60-0

Copyright © 2016 Amy Giustino Talbot All Rights Reserved.

Original Illustrations:
Christina Havens

Front Cover Photo:
Samantha DeLeon Photography

Author Headshot:
Christie Connell – Azure Photo Studio

Disclaimer:
This book is designed to provide information about the subject matter covered. The opinions expressed in this book are those of the author, not the publisher. Every effort has been made to make this book as complete and as accurate as possible. However, there may be mistakes both typographical and in content. Therefore, this text should be used only as a general guide and not as the ultimate source of information. The author and publisher of this book shall have neither liability nor responsibility to any person or entity with respect to any loss or damage caused or alleged to be caused directly or indirectly by the information contained in this book.

Printed in the United States of America

Dedication

My Zen Babies,
Olivia, Luke and Sierra,
Thank you for choosing me to be your mom.

Paul,
I am eternally grateful for this crazy life
we've created together.

Dad,
There are not enough words in this world to express my
gratitude for your unconditional support.

I love you all to the moon and back forever.
xxoo

Finding and Maintaining Your Zen While Surviving Life with Young Children

My daughter recently asked me, "Mommy, what is it like to be a Mom?"

I thought about it for a minute.

"Honey, it's like going to the best party ever, except when it's over, you don't get to leave with your friends. You have to stay to clean up—*alone*."

And so it is with being a parent.

My best friend has one kid. She can travel around the world. Literally. I have three, and I successfully travel around town. On a daily basis I need to remind myself that one day, I will, in fact, miss the constant state of chaos.

Maybe? Probably!

So, who am I? And what makes me think I'm qualified to write a book on becoming a zen parent?

I am you. I'm your girlfriend, your sister, your next-door neighbor. We are all the same. We have all made the decision (consciously or subconsciously) to teach a child the guidelines for this crazy thing we call life. We are all zen at the core of our being. I am hoping this guide will help you find the perfect *balance* to reclaim it.

Today, I am a mom. I am a Nutritionist, Reiki Master, and Karuna® Reiki Practitioner. I am a daily seeker of zen, a yoga student, and a student of life. I lose my cool, misplace my peace. Sometimes I forget to put my son's shoes on before we go to the store. I often turn the car around because I've left my purse at home. But, that's not who I am. That's the result of being completely entrenched in this wonderful and chaotic life I have chosen.

I am an evolving spirit searching for peace and enlightenment every day, not only for my own sanity, but to set the best example for my children.

In life before kids, I had a career that didn't involve the humans I made. I happily worked my days and nights away. I traveled, taught, saw clients. I was inspired to go to work. I have a Bachelor's degree in Foods and Nutrition. I was really good at my job. I was the one who went into the offices of healthcare practitioners and helped them to integrate nutrition, supplements, and nutrition education into their practices. Fun, right?

One day, this little person entered (well, *exited* my body . . . *entered* my life) and everything changed. I changed. There was nothing more important than this little girl. I told my husband that there was no way I could leave her to start traveling again. Being the accepting man that he is, he understood that this meant a bigger burden for him to financially care for our growing family, but that my work at home was important at this time.

I was blessed to be able to walk away from a successful career so that I could spend every day watching this awesome, powerful little person unfold before my very eyes. Then came her amazing brother, and a couple years later, a spunky little sister, too.

Yup, you counted right; three kids in four years (yes, I'm insane, I mean zen, I mean yikes!!)

I am so awed by the fact that I am able to call them my family, my kids. And here's what the decision to be *just* a mom has taught me: Kids are born zen. This crazy world they are born into zaps their zen. It's our job as their parents to find peace ourselves so they can learn to re-zen themselves.

Zen is the balance of body, mind, and spirit. Finding my Zen, my inner calm, was the ultimate challenge of my life and is something I still consciously work on pretty much daily. Living a zen existence involves making conscious choices to live a more peaceful and accepting life.

I started out seriously appalled by myself—and how I couldn't get my act together. I went from feeling like I had this Mommy thing down, to being certain that my children were going to be emotionally scarred for life by my sudden inability to get them to school on time.

It took me three kids to figure out that using a nursing cover was not going to smother my baby; nor was my baby going to come to any other kind of harm from using one. I nursed my first two babies in my car for fear that my failure to figure out a nursing cover meant failure as a parent—and everyone around me would see my failure.

Baby # 3 brought a whole new ballgame. I fought the nursing cover, and I won! My first two babies were very close in age, so running back to the car was no big deal, and neither was staying home. Once baby three arrived, neither running to the car nor staying home were options any longer. With two active preschoolers, play dates, gymnastics, soccer, basketball, and way too much energy for any of our own good, we had to be on-the-go, with baby sister in tow.

This book is a tool to help us (those of us with a minimum of one kid ruling our life) regain a bit of sanity. For those who have ever thought: These things only happen to me! I can assure you, it is not *you*.

Craziness happens to all of us!

You are *never* alone.

1

Co-Parenting

No Snowflake ever falls in the wrong place
— Zen Proverb

Your child did not arrive here by accident. You chose someone to make them with. Everything is exactly as it was meant to be.

Single Parents.

If you are a single parent reading this: Namaste!

I bow to you. I am in awe of you. How you do it is beyond my realm of consciousness. Raising people is scary! It involves an intricate list of do's and do not's. Sharing the misery and joys with someone else is great because you have someone to point the finger at when your child exhibits some strange behavior. If there is an option and your child's other parent is of healthy mind and spirit, I would always recommend co-parenting; even if you are no longer in a relationship with said other parent. With that said, here's what I have learned from co-parenting.

Early Years.

The early years seems to last FOR-freaking-EVER. But, in the big picture, they go by in the blink of an eye. Hard as it may be, do your best to not wish them away.

Some days, I am literally standing at the door with one kid in my arms and one wrapped around each leg, waiting for my husband to take these people, so I can leave to find an hour of sanity. If you can, DO IT! Run fast and run hard until you get to the car.

Get in and get out of there as quickly as humanly possible before someone gets the door open and starts chasing your car down the street screaming "MAMA, DON'T GO!" Then you have to stop the car, bring the child back into the house, feel guilty, etc. KNEES TO NOSE! Get outta there! Go anywhere you feel calm. Sit in the car and listen to anything other than Radio Disney. Go to Target and listen to the choir of Angels sing as the sliding doors open and you enter kid-free. Do nothing. Do anything. Just be. Trust me, you deserve this.

Partners.

I promise it is not your partner's goal to annoy you or to make you feel crazier than you already do—it only seems that way. Give it two to three years, and this feeling will subside. Unless you have another kid, then it's back to square one.

Dads, fear not! Mom will not hate you forever. Promise! You did this to her. Once the pain goes away and she has a few hours of sleep under her belt, she'll forget how much she hates you. And she just may go back to liking you, too. I said **maybe**.

Mom—Your sex drive *will* return—one day. I can't say which day, but one day in the not so distant future, you will feel like having sex again. Just remember that's how you got into this boat in the first place, so be responsible.

Relinquish a pinch of control.

Have a Honey-Do List—at least for the projects that you don't have a timeline on. Also, have a "I'll do it my damn self-list" for that stuff you really want done in a timely fashion. If it really needs to be done your way . . . do it yourself. Seriously. No one is going to do it the way you want it done. Get over expecting people to read your mind and do it your way.

When someone asks if they can help, say Hell YES without feeling any guilt whatsoever. I know, I know . . . it's SO darn difficult. But, occasionally relinquish control and trust that getting it done is enough. Even if it's not done your way (aka: the right way).

Take care of one another. It's so easy getting caught up with the kids and their needs that you forget your partner could use a little of that energy and compassion, too.

Steppin' Out.

It may sound simple, but date night is actually quite important. There is a wonderful feeling that overcomes me each time I sit down at a restaurant with my husband alone. I don't have to situate anyone but myself in a seat. I don't have to play *I Spy* or find anything to occupy anyone, but myself. It's liberating and reminds me that I can still interact in the world without a person attached to my body.

Working to make money is imperative, but remember, you're also living this particular life just this once. Some of us are so busy making a living that we forget to live our life.

Parenting is as much a partnership as marriage. Regardless of what is happening in your romantic relationship, when it comes to your co-parenting kids, be on the same side. Kids are slippery little suckers. Stick together.

Exercises:

1. Write a letter to your child remembering the first thing you noticed about your partner. Tell them one trait you hope they get from your partner and one you hope they get from you. Go on to tell them your hopes and dreams for their future.

2. The human mind is like water in a lake. When it is restless, it gets muddy and becomes hard to see clearly. If you let it settle, things become much clearer. Clarity of mind helps to improve communication skills and brings about more creativity. Commit to trying guided meditation for one week at bedtime or first thing in the morning before you get out of bed. Nothing crazy, not too long. Just google meditation for relaxation or meditation for parents, sit back or lie down, and let the magic happen. The worst thing that can happen is that you spent a few minutes of your day focusing on yourself and becoming more relaxed. The best thing is that you have created a daily habit that clears your mind and helps you in every aspect of your life (no pressure though).

3. Create an "I'll do it my damn self" list of things that need to be done that you can do for yourself without your partner's help. Then go take one inspired-action step toward completing that list.

The Zen Parent Guide

Affirmations

I live a life full of gratitude.

I am grateful for all the love around me.

I am strong and resilient.

I can handle anything that comes my way.

2

Ease Up (on yourself and everyone around you)

The only zen you find at the top of the mountain is the zen you bring with you. — *Zen Proverb*

We, as parents, are under more pressure than a kid trying to stay off the naughty list at Christmas. We must be honest, respectful, calm, and energetic all the while acting as teachers, master negotiators, psychiatrists, house keepers, launderers, drivers, and so much more! It's intense. It's also impossible. We have little eyes on us all the time, little minds like sponges ready to absorb all we model for them, little ears just waiting to repeat that one curse word that slips out as you spill your delicious coffee all over the car. All this to say—let it be what it will be.

Just a reminder: These little years go by in a flash. It may seem like a lifetime, but it's really very short in the grand scheme of things. You'll look back one day and realize that it's been gone longer than it lasted. Take advantage of each sweet little cuddle you can steal, even if that cuddle happens to be at 4:00 a.m.

Be present.

The future will come, I promise. Embrace now. Your kids will be young only once. Embrace it. If you're slinging cereal and changing diapers all day long, own it. You don't have to like every second of it but love it nonetheless. One day, your kid will think they're all that and a bag of chips. Right now, you're cool, and they need you. Let yourself love being needed.

Your kids will poop, puke, and pee on you because they love you! Well, that's what we tell ourselves to feel better about the daily dose of excrement on our clothing. You're not the first person to walk into your older child's school with puke on your shoulder—and I can assure you, you won't be the last.

Get. Over. It.

You will have issues with your first child that seem comical with the subsequent ones . . . I was seriously certain my first baby might actually suffocate in the nursing cover. Should you have a second child, you will laugh at the former you and how your first child never touched the floor as your second eats dirt. Your first only had organic food. Your second gets table food as soon as they get teeth. Your first slept in her crib at four weeks. Your second never left your bed because you were too tired to take them back after the midnight feeding. It's all good, and if it works for you and it works for the rest of the family, then it just works.

The *Baby Einstein* you played for your first likely didn't actually make them smarter, so don't feel guilty that you were too tired to do it for the rest. (Or that you couldn't find the DVD, and then someone called and you checked the caller ID and decided to ignore the call because you were about to do something . . . what was I looking for again???)

Forget remembering what you were doing if you get distracted. I'm not sure if or when this comes back, but I'm over eight years in and still suffer from CRS—Can't Remember S**t.

Everyone forgets.

No need to feel guilty that you confuse your children's schedules, names, birthdays, weights, or which one did what when. What you won't ever forget is how much you love each of them . . . and which one was colicky! THAT you won't EVER forget!

Feeling overwhelmed?

Don't forget to breathe . . . if you're feeling like you might actually explode, check to be sure you're actually breathing. Do it—Right now. If yoga has taught me anything, it's the importance of actually breathing. It is maybe our most vital life function, and while, yes, your body does this innately, sometimes a good cleansing breath can truly calm your mind.

Play nice.

What's with parents? Moms especially! We are so hard on ourselves and one another. It has been my personal mission to stop judging and start trying to understand why other mothers make the decisions they do. It is far too easy to judge others for doing things differently than we do.

My question to myself is always: "Is that better than the way I do it?"

Sometimes the answer is: "Woo Hoo! That's the best thing since sliced bread!" Sometimes the answer is: "She's gone bat s**t crazy!" Either way, it is for me to observe and not for me to judge another parent's decision. Honestly, if another parenting style works for their family, and it's not affecting you or your kids, then what does it matter anyway?

I'm originally from New Jersey. We totally call it as we see it. Sometimes this comes across as judgment. I often need to check in with myself before I speak to be sure I'm not passing judgment, but rather simply stating an observation as I see it without critique.

When we begin our path to zen, we can sometimes go a little "cray cray" and fall back into our old habits of criticizing and feeling insecure or superior. Should this happen, be kind to yourself. But, never, ever let your kids see this. These are your opinions, your beliefs, not your child's. Keep that stuff to your own self.

Forgive.

I'm no expert, but I think it takes quite a lot to scar your children for life, so ease up on yourself. If you lose your head and yell a little too much or a little too loudly for something small because you're angry with your partner or stressed about money, just say you're sorry. Your kids will forgive you. Forgive yourself.

Forgive yourself. Forgive others.

You are not your past. You are not your mistakes. According to the late and magical Dr. Wayne Dyer, "You are an infinite spiritual being having a temporary human experience." So is everyone around you. Defining yourself or others by errors is neither fair nor productive.

Forgiving yourself for not being perfect is really a gift for the whole family. Be kind to yourself and let your kids see you doing it. What more awesome gift can you give them to let them know that it's cool to be kind . . . to yourself?

Your children think you're perfect. They don't know (nor should they) that you weigh 20 pounds more than you'd like or that you cannot stand the way your hair is falling today or that your skin is just a mess. All they see is the perfect person who loves and nurtures them. So, why in the world would we show or tell them anything differently?

Our children identify themselves by the way we identify ourselves. I can't think of a better reason to find it within ourselves to be ok with the way we are right now. You don't have to love it. You don't even have to accept it, but you must keep it to yourself. Strive for positive change for health and fitness. Show your kids what a healthy, strong person looks like. They do not need your issues on their minds or bodies.

Don't make your insecurities and issues theirs. They belong to you and are yours to deal with. Kids have enough to deal with while figuring out who THEY are—so don't add to it.

Moms.

Learning to love your post-baby body is a challenge. Anyone who looks awesome after 5 or 6 weeks is a freak of nature and certainly NOT the norm . . . In general, I go with a FULL 9 months up and FULL 9 months down. Realistically, that's how long it took you to gain that weight. Take the pressure off yourself to fit into your skinny jeans with a 3-month old. That said, I have been known to take a year (or longer) to get back to my pre-baby weight. If you're over 35, just get over it right now. Even if you *do* get back to your pre-baby weight, nothing, and I do mean nothing, will be where it was before. Damn you, gravity!

Try to avoid the *Grass is Greener Syndrome*. Difficult as it may be, don't compare. The truth is we can't truly know what path anyone else is on. Maybe they have come through a problematic past, or are going through a challenging situation behind closed doors, or are headed for difficulty. We just never know what anyone else has had to or will have to deal with. The grass may look greener, but it could be artificial turf.

Be Kind.

Be kind to yourself. Be kind to others. I'm not saying allow others to behave badly toward you. I'm saying be kind enough to yourself to know when to walk away and when to stay.

Speaking of behaving badly . . . let's chat for a moment on toxic people. Your children should never have to watch you suffer through a toxic relationship. You are their teacher and inner voice. They identify themselves by the way you see yourself and the way you allow others to treat you. Therefore, for your children's' sake, you don't ever have to feel guilty about removing negative people from your life. No matter who that person is: a relative, partner, colleague, friend, or someone you just met. You have the power to remove people from your life who cause pain or make you feel less than the amazing person you are.

Now, if said toxic person owns up to their behavior and makes an honest and sincere effort to change, it is also good to demonstrate for your children the art of forgiveness. But, if a person disregards your feelings, ignores your boundaries, and continues to treat you or your children in a harmful or disrespectful way, they need to get the boot. Empower your children to take charge of their relationships and show them what a respectful relationship looks like.

Making a mistake is not the end of the world.

Seriously, it's not.

Exercises:

1. Write down three things you love about yourself, three things you love about your life, and three things you WILL forgive yourself for as of this moment.

2. Take an honest, mental inventory of the people in your life. Is there anyone who you or your children feel badly or negative around? Is there anyone that you feel exhausted after spending time with? Maybe they have a cynical or jaded perspective on life? Maybe they are just insecure and that shows up in their words or behaviors. Now, ask yourself: how would my life feel if I didn't have to deal with the feelings, emotions, and heaviness I'm getting from this relationship? If thoughts of being free of them make you feel happier and lighter, more peaceful, maybe you start limiting time spent with them. Maybe you should start spending more time with people you feel light and happy around. Maybe you just took the first step toward a brighter, more positive you!

3. Take a moment today to compliment another parent. It doesn't matter what you're giving them kudos for. Watch their reaction. Their face may light up, they may blush a little, or they may completely deny the compliment you just threw their way. Do it anyway. Somewhere deep inside each of us, acceptance and reassurance that we are doing something . . . anything. . . right is necessary. Take note of how good you feel when expressing positivity toward your peer. Now, take that feeling and apply it back to yourself. You're doing great, and I'm so grateful to be in this beautiful, crazy world, co-parenting with YOU!

Amy Giustino Talbot

Affirmations

Everything is exactly as it should be.
All is right in my world.

I forgive those that have harmed me.
I forgive myself.
I peacefully detach from the pain.

Today, I am overflowing with joy and gratitude.

I have a strong heart and a clear mind.

3

Take Care of You, Kid.

The Trouble is You Think You Have Time.
— Zen Proverb

If you don't believe in and care for yourself, who will? We set the example our children will live by for the rest of their lives. Treat yourself as you want them to treat themselves.

Give up the guilt.

On more than one occasion, I've been guilty of feeling guilty. The guilt I'm talking about is the guilt of taking care of me. I will skip my chiropractic appointment that will help my aching back because it's not in the budget. But my back is aching because one of my kids slept on my pillow and the other on my legs. We go without because we want our kids to have everything. What we need to learn is that taking care of yourself only helps you to better care for them.

Find your Village.

It takes a village—I've said it before. I'm saying it again: Accept Help! Take it from a "doer." I get how hard this is but just try it once! You'll feel so much better once some of the pressure is off, and that next time it will be a little easier to ask. Every mom needs someone she can count on. I am blessed with multiple someones, and I'm sure if you think about it, you will find you are, too.

Have some friend time (*maybe with some members of your village*). Go out. Get dressed in clothes that don't have some sort of kid stain on them. Have an adult conversation. Feel normal. This will do wonders for your brain; especially if you are certain, as I have been many times, that it is actually disintegrating in there.

Coffee (or some other delightful beverage that you cannot share with your children).

Coffee dates back to the 13th century, where I am certain it was invented by a mom! Don't ever let anyone tell you differently. Also, there's now research suggesting coffee has actual health benefits. If someone questions your coffee intake, you should immediately stop speaking to that person. You do not have time for that kind of negativity in your life. Drinking coffee with a member of your village makes it even better for your mind, body and spirit. (I think?)

Do it for yourself.

Find some "Me Time." This is the time that you only do things for yourself—and no one else. You're reading this book, so maybe you've already got this covered, good job! Now, keep up the good work.

Find something you love to do just for yourself and do it.

I love yoga. I feel calm and peaceful when I practice. I find my zen while I am there. My fave pose is *savasana* (the little snooze at the end). It's me-time. And my kids actually are so excited to hear about my yoga class when I get home. It gives us a little extra convo time when I return home all zenned out.

Treat YOUR body well.

Teach your children to make healthy, conscious choices about food, exercise, and meditation. And by teach, I mean DO IT and lead them by example.

Healthy eating is necessary to help prevent disease in the body, but it is also to nourish the soul and revitalize your energy. Eating food in a form closer to its natural state will truly help to raise your energy. Refined or processed foods will not nourish as well as natural foods.

Eat protein. It will hold you over longer than carbs and help to rebuild that muscle you lost while sitting on the couch exhausted from carrying that little person in your body for ten months.

Aim for protein at each meal and snack. It will keep you feeling full longer, help to build muscle—which will burn more fat, which will make you feel better. Oh, and it helps balance your blood sugar, as an added bonus. So, you shouldn't get that 3 p.m. coffee crash. (You know what I'm talkin' about.)

Act like a cow and graze . . . small meals and snacks throughout the day to keep your energy up.

Healthy, smart fats are essential to good health. Nuts, olive and other vegetable oils, flax, sesame seeds, avocado, and fish are some examples. Good fats speed up your metabolism and are essential for fat burning. They also play an integral part in immune and brain function. Wouldn't you say brain function is important in parenting?

Use breastfeeding as a way to practice healthy habits. Sure, you get so hungry you could eat your kitchen table but choose celery with almond butter instead. Same consistency as the kitchen table, just more nutritious! Yes, for many, breastfeeding hurts. Duh. There's a person latching onto the tender skin of your freaking nipple. You will fill up with milk when someone else's baby cries in a store—gotta love nature. You will be attached to your child for months but isn't that what you signed up for when you got pregnant? All you need to do is try (if you are physically able). Breastfeeding for any amount of time—one day is better than no days—is truly a gift for your child. Breastmilk is organic fast food for babies, and it's also great on the budget. By the way, it's also the actual biological use for your boobies.

There, I said it!

If you want to look and feel like a million bucks, you can't be eating off the dollar menu.

Buy organic, all-natural or local, wherever possible. Reducing the amount of unnatural substances (*ickies*, as we call 'em) in these little bodies, which are already dealing with more environmental toxins in one day than we did in weeks when we were kids, can only help.

While we are on *ickies*—my suggestion is to reduce the amount (of *ickies*) you take in at home. As a rule of thumb, keep most of the foods in your home as close to their natural state as possible, i.e. real potatoes, instead of fries or potato chips. This way, when you are out, you can let loose a bit and have something you don't normally keep in your house. This will increase the number of nutrients your children (and you) take in and decrease the empty calories.

I am certainly not suggesting that you ban all treats from your house or that you never indulge in the delicious delights this world has to offer. I am simply proposing doing everything in moderation. Balance in all. Got it? K. Good.

Think positive.

Always try to see the best in people. If you're always thinking the world is against you, you will wind up raising world-weary kids—and that isn't in anyone's best interest.

When all else fails and you just can't get your zen on, I highly recommend finding a good therapist. Therapy is not just for crazy people anymore. Seeking therapy is a sign of strength and desire to do better for yourself and the peeps who count on you. A quality therapy session can, in most cases, help you sort out your emotions.

 *Exercises:*

1. *Go to the food store and buy healthy food for you to eat. Not for the kids, not for your partner, your parents, or anyone else whose health you've been putting before yourself. Put your own physical needs on the forefront of your mind (just this once).*

2. *Start today. Do something just for you. Take a little me time. Doesn't have to be hours, take five minutes. Take an hour. Whatever you can squeeze into your busy parent life. Last night I sat on the floor and gave myself a pedicure because it's summer, my feet are downright embarrassing, and I just can't seem to find the time to get to the nail salon. Today, I'm sitting here writing this exercise for you. I may only be able to write for ten minutes because, as I'm thinking this thought, someone is calling "Mommy!" Do whatever you can squeeze in for you that you have been putting off or ignoring because someone else always needs SOMEthing!*

3. *Shower Power. During your next shower, imagine the water washing over you taking away all of your stress, anxieties, doubts, and concerns. Shampoo out all the fears, worries, and regrets that need to be cleaned out of your head. Have a good cry if you feel it. Let it all come up, and then let all those negative emotions swirl down the drain. Condition back in the self-love, peace, and softness you so richly deserve.*

Amy Giustino Talbot

Affirmations

Today, I commit to treating myself well.
I am worthy of my own love and attention.

I love myself, exactly as I am.

I am strong and resilient.

My mind and heart are filled
with compassion and courage.

4

Taking Care of Business

When Walking, Walk. When Eating, Eat.
- Zen Proverb

When Parenting. Parent.

Set expectations, not limitations.

It's been said, and I highly agree, that the only limits in life are the ones you make. Is *your* limited thinking limiting the abundance of your reality? Is *your* limited thinking affecting the way you parent?

It doesn't matter how many kids you have, we are all steering through this parenthood process. We need to stick together, but that doesn't mean you just decide to let someone else parent your kid because you don't feel like being the "*bad guy*." Be strong. Be fit. Take care of your business . . . the right way.

Showing your kids that it's ok to be wrong is totally awesome. Showing them what to do to rectify the situation is even better. An apology is not a sign of weakness. It's a sign of strength

Listen closely to your kids, but not too closely to adults.

Listen. Truly listen to your child when they speak. Giving them the gift of our attention is something more valuable than any toy we can buy. Hearing them and their stories makes them feel understood and significant. Who doesn't want to feel understood and significant, right? A child who feels important and understood by their parent when they are small is one who is more likely to turn to that parent when they are older and their issues are much bigger.

Wouldn't it be smashing if we could read our kids' minds? Well, we can't. So make announcements, such as:

(in your best drill sergeant tone)

WE ARE LEAVING THIS HOUSE IN 10 MINUTES! IF THERE IS ANYTHING YOU NEED TO DO OR GET, DO SO NOW! OTHERWISE, ASSEMBLE AT THE CAR! ONCE WE HAVE LEFT THE DRIVEWAY, I DO NOT WANT TO HEAR ANOTHER WORD ABOUT WHAT YOU WANT OR FORGOT!

Gaining advice from others.

There are two kinds of advice: solicited and unsolicited. Everyone has their own version of "wisdom" to share. You **really** don't need to accept all that is offered. Whether you are looking to others for guidance or it is given by those well-intentioned—or by sometimes unwittingly judgmental folks in your life—there is one commonality. What works for some, does not necessarily work for you. Take it all with a grain of salt and always, always, always go with your intuition. Following your gut will continually lead you in the right direction.

Crying it out.

Gasp! She spoke of the illicit topic! Works for some; it did not for us. My strong-willed kids screamed to the point that I was exhausted *for* them. I personally think I actually did scar my first daughter for life by doing it—and to this day, she's STILL not a good sleeper! My opinion: Go with what feels right for you and your baby. Only you know what that is exactly. Don't be afraid to try new or different things in order to figure it out. Give it three nights of any chosen method and then see where you are.

Co-sleeping.

Gulp. Another gaffe topic! Many think it's crazy. Many think there's no other way to do it. Personally, I adore listening to my little snorers as they sleep. Again, only YOU know what's right for YOUR family. Anyone who tells you that their kids have never slept in their bed is either trying to make you feel like a freak for the fact that yours do, or they're lying—probably both. Ignore them.

Fear.

We fear letting them down. We fear scarring them for life. We fear not setting the right boundaries that will keep them from becoming tyrants later in life (or earlier). Fear is good. Fear helps us to be better parents.

Every single one of us has had one (or many) of those "I am the worst parent in the world" moments. In these moments, you are certain that you have done irreparable damage to your children because you flipped your shit over something small or because they Just. Would. Not. Go. To. SLEEP! Kids are resilient. Say you're sorry. Kiss and make up. Forgive yourself, and they will forgive you.

If you've had more than one, your first child seems tougher because they were strong enough to survive being your guinea pig. After all, there's no handbook (*until now, wink wink*). You and your first born are on a wild adventure together . . . running blindly though the days, flying by the seat of your pants, figuring it out as you go. That's the deal with the first. They signed on for that when they came into this world. No guilt required, at least not on this one.

Find your calm.

The calmer (the true internal zen-kinda calm) you become, the calmer (the true, internal zen-kinda calm) your families will become. This is true. I know it to be so because I've been that crazy, stressed, lunatic mom, and I've been the true internal zen mom—and my whole family responded in kind to both.

Everyone cries, darling.

Kids cry and sometimes they cry and they cry and they cry. I can't remember the last day in my life that didn't contain tears (sometimes mine, sometimes theirs). There's a difference between crying for a true need, crying out of frustration or fear, and crying to get what you want. We, as parents, need to know when to legitimately acknowledge those tears as a need and when to disregard them as a desperate act of attention. THIS is one of the most difficult aspects of parenting, especially with a preschooler: knowing when you're being played and when you're truly needed. All I can say is: *"May the Force be with you."*

You are in good company.

I Repeat and I repeat and I repeat . . .

Repeating yourself is every parent's burden to bear. It's not fair and pretty much sucks, but it's ours to keep. I promise you are NOT the only parent in the world repeating yourself to the point that you're actually exhausted listening to the sound of your own voice!

You can do it all.

Take each day as a new beginning, a fresh slate. Try to leave yesterday there and start today making the best choices for you and your kids. You feel like you can't do it all, but I assure you—you can and you will. Multi-tasking will save your life. There were many times that I would have a baby on the boob, a cup of coffee on the counter, and be packing school lunches with my free hand. It is truly amazing what you can accomplish with one hand, while the other is occupying a fussy baby.

Get those sillies out.

Children are wonderfully resilient. Their energy can be intoxicating, sometimes invigorating, and often exhausting. Remember when you were a kid and were so excited for something that you could barely contain yourself? Try to find that within yourself and then take them somewhere to get it all out—outdoor park, bounce park, pool—anywhere they can GET-IT-OUT.

What's up, Doc?

Let's talk doctors for a moment, shall we? It is your job to be fiercely smart when it comes to your child's health. Be well-versed and make informed decisions about everything you put into your child. In 2000, The World Health Organization ranked the United States 38th. Yes, you read that right THIRTY EIGHTH in the world for overall health. Let's change that by making *the* best, most educated decisions we can for our children's health.

Never feel bad or out of place for questioning your doctor. This is YOUR child. Take decisions regarding their health very personally. Make it your business to understand everything that your doctor is saying or doing to your child. You are their voice—and their one and only advocate. A doctor may be an expert in health, but you must be the expert of *your* child's health. You are in charge of their health decisions. So stay educated.

No is a complete sentence.

If something that is happening in your child's world doesn't feel right to you, then the answer is a resounding NO! It doesn't matter if you can't explain your reasoning or if your child's doctor or anyone else is insisting you are wrong. If it feels wrong, it probably is. Go with that.

You deserve a pat on the back.

Be proud of yourself when you're proud of your kids. Especially when they do something that you've tried to instill in them for what seems like FOREVER and you were certain they were ignoring you. They hear you . . . even when you think they're not listening.

Exercises:

1. Just BE for a full ten minutes. Focus on your breath. Breathe deeply in through your nose and out through your mouth five times. Continue to consciously breathe now, but calmly. Each time your mind wanders away from your breath, gently redirect it to the sound of inhaling peace, exhaling stress. Let go. There is nothing to do and nowhere to be, but here. Take these few moments to Be calm. Be relaxed. Do nothing. Allow the wave of relaxation to wash over you and help you drift off to sleep or move on with your day wrapped in a blanket of allowing.

2. As parents, we receive a lot of wisdom from others. Often, we feel obligated to entertain it all. Make a conscious choice as to which pieces to keep and which to toss out. Assess the value of the advice given based on things like: how well their kids turned out and how they present the recommendation. What unspoken vibes did you get when the advice was given? Did you get tense? Did your head begin to hurt? Did you feel this was given in love or out of judgment for the way you were doing it that they deemed wrong? Did you feel good and light? Use this to determine whether this was good guidance for you—and if it works with your parenting style. Be candid with yourself. No one is listening to your thoughts, but you.

3. It can often feel that we are in a state of constant instructing, raising our voices or speaking in tones that even we don't appreciate. For one week, try using affirmations of good behavior in lieu of negative statements when correcting behavior. For example, your child is playing with their food. Using this technique, you might say, "I really love it when you eat like a big kid." Or your child is being unkind to a sibling—this would be addressed by saying, "I really appreciate it when you show kindness to your siblings." Or your child is screaming. Your reaction might be to let them know you really like when they use the same tone they would like you to use toward them. Where you might want to flip out, it actually makes the child stop in their tracks and say, "Oh, OK." I've found my kids react in kind when I use this technique. They may just be in shock, but whatever works.

The Zen Parent Guide

Affirmations

I am exactly what my child needs me to be.
My child is exactly as I need them to be.

Today, I leave my old thought patterns behind and take up new, more positive ones.

I release everything in me that is holding me back from my true greatness.

I am enough.

5

Nurturing Them Doesn't Mean Enabling Bad Behavior

Experience this moment to the fullest.
– Zen Proverb

Look and Listen.

The quieter you become, the more you can hear. Listen. Listen to your inner guiding system. It is always right.

Every once in a while, I like to take a step back and really look at the people I am raising. Is their behavior something I'm proud of? Are they turning out the way I dreamed? Are they nice to other kids? Do they respect adults? If so, I pat myself on the back and go about my business. Try it. And be honest with yourself. If you find that your children are not turning out the way you had hoped they would, ask yourself—what can/should I be doing differently to stop the insanity? How can I help mold and unfold the true potential of my children?

Shine like a Star for your kids.

Be an example of the kind of adult you want your child to become. They learn first and foremost by watching you.

Teaching your children kindness, compassion and tolerance, in my humble opinion, is as important as academics. The more you deal with their issues in a gentle way, the more they will deal with their own issues and other people's issues compassionately. Empathy can be taught. We, as parents, truly lead by example, and these kids will emulate every-single-minute-thing we do. One of the greatest gifts we can give them is to show them how to handle situations or people, even negative ones in a positive way.

Kids are sponges. Speak to your children the way you want them to speak to you . . . and the way you want them to represent you. Sounds simple enough, but sometimes it's simply overlooked. Trust me. Everything you say WILL be repeated.

Raise 'em right.

You don't ever want to be *that* Mom . . . the one with *those* kids; the ones who inevitably come up in every conversation amongst your group of friends because they cannot comprehend how such an awesome person can be raising such awful children! Do yourself, your children, and the rest of the world a favor; Raise 'em right! When they leave your house, the rest of the world has to deal with them, so lovingly teach them respect and gratitude.

Excuses are like garbage cans—everyone has one and they all stink! Don't make excuses for bad behavior. Correct it, kindly! Would you want your child taking care of you in your old age? If not, put yourself in time out or enlist the help of someone who knows—and figure out how to introduce more empathy into their lives.

Love, love and more love.

Kiss your kids and tell them you love them every day . . . particularly when they're in trouble or making you CRAZYYYYY!

Never underestimate the healing power of love. When you're starting to feel like you're going to crack and all you want to do is scream, take a moment, take a breath (*I know, here I go with the breathing again*) and hug them. Hug them long and hug them with all the love in your heart because their bad behavior may just be a cry for a little extra love that they don't know how to express. It could also be age-appropriate acting out. You have to figure that one out. But, if the hug doesn't turn things around, a time-out or loss of a privilege might just be the right thing. Always start with the love.

Mother's Instinct.

It's real. Go with your gut, always! That's all I need to say about that.

Exercises:

1. Take an honest and non-judgmental look at how your children interact with one another, their friends and other adults. Are they interacting or behaving in a way that makes you proud? Are they kind? This is an exercise of compassion, and a reality check for ways you may want to reevaluate or course-correct your parenting style or the examples you're setting. Please no judging of them or yourself. Just truly look and evaluate if your parenting choices maybe need a few creative ways to bring more compassion to their lives? Jot down a few things you would like to do differently in your parenting style.

2. Go tell your kids you love them just as they are. Tell them you're so happy they chose you to be their parent. Give them an example of one thing they do that makes you so proud. Watch their reaction. Do they light up? Do they deny or shy away from the compliment? Do they hug you? These can all be very good indicators of how they are feeling about themselves. Being aware of how our children feel about themselves can help you better understand their behavior. If they shy away or deny your compliment, continue the conversation to find the source of their insecurity. If they beam and thank you, it's a good indicator that your child's self-esteem is in a good place, at least in this moment.

3. Children are like flower buds waiting to blossom into beautiful blooms. Get a pen out and make notes of the ways you can help them to become who they are here to be without putting your own wants and desires on them. We can help them unfold without molding them simply by taking their interests, goals, and loves and guiding them in the right direction to make their dreams a reality. Does your child love to write or draw? Purchase them a pen and paper set or a set of colored pencils and a sketch pad. Does your child love to be active? Sign them up for soccer, gymnastics, basketball, etc. There are all kinds of cost effective options through the parks and rec systems or through coupons now. Look into it. Get them involved.

The Zen Parent Guide

Affirmations

I am a strong and positive influence in my child's life.
Nurturing them is a gift to me and the whole world.

My child is like a flower bud waiting to bloom.
They are perfect exactly where they are.

I continue to grow and change as my child does.
I have the power to be anything I choose.
I choose happy.

My child is unique and special.
I love and support them in all of their dreams,
regardless of society's definition of
normal or acceptable.

6

Energy of a Child

Knowledge is learning something every day.
Wisdom is letting go of something every day.
– Zen Proverb

Ernest Holmes said, "Where the mind goes, the energy flows." Where is your mind taking your energy?

How often do you sit back and watch your kids thinking, "If I only had an ounce of their energy, I'd . . ."? Well, we may be older, more mature (*some of us, anyway*), and our bodies may be a little more weathered, but we should always strive to find ways to get as close to that energy as we can. And we certainly need to help our kids keep as much of their energy as they can. They'll need it in this progressive world they are growing up in!

Balance.

It's worth a seventh or eighth reminder that it is our responsibility as parents to set the best examples for our kids. This is of particular importance when it comes to taking care of the body vessel. After all, do as I say, not as I do rarely flies anymore. Demonstrate and teach balance.

Drink water every single day.

The average human body is made up of about 60% water. The brain is around 70%–73% water. The lungs are over 80%. Water even helps digest our food and transport nutrients (HELLO… Energy) through the body and waste out of the body. If you're not hydrating, how can the body function? How can you feel energetic? *Drink water!*

Vitamins and minerals are your friends. Take them with WATER. With the stressful world we live in, depleted soil sources and the day to day nutrient-depleting lifestyles we lead, be kind to yourself and get 'em wherever you can.

Get grounded.

Send your kids outside barefoot to put their feet in the grass when they are making you crazy. It will ground them. Then take a few deep breaths (*ugh, will I just stop with the breathing?*) and go play in the grass with them. It will ground you, too.

Moms are Magic.

Children see magic because they look for it. They believe it is there. They believe you are magic. They believe the world is full of magic. The only person keeping you from believing in a little magic is you. You have the power.

Exercises:

1. Commit to one inspired action you will take today with your children and/or partner. For example, sit together and talk about your day. Ask about theirs. Say one thing you are grateful for; say one thing you love about one another. Talk about or do something that is positive, uplifting, and brings up a sense of gratitude for each of you.

2. Take a dip in the water. If you don't have access to an ocean, lake or river, then make it a bath with sea salts or Epsom salts. Take a break, clear your energy, and raise your vibration.

3. Sit on the floor with your kids (or even better, all by your peaceful lonesome) and do a little stretching. Sit in a straddle and reach for each ankle. Raise your hands above your head and reach for the sky. Put one hand on the ground next to your bottom and reach the other toward the sky, then switch. Feel your tight muscles relax as you slowly move through a series of stretches. Notice how good it feels when you stand up now that your muscles have some oxygen pumping through them. Try this every day for a week. Take note of how the tension in your body decreases over time.

The Zen Parent Guide

Affirmations

I am full of sparkle and compassion and everything wonderful in the universe.

I fully participate in filling my day with hope, health, and joy.

**I am grounded and peaceful.
I am raising grounded and peaceful children.
I am whole just as I am.**

Finding Your Zen . . . And Theirs

Breathe Mindfully & Smile Peacefully.

Whatever you believe about yourself on the inside is what you will manifest in your external life. Allow yourself to believe that you are a beautiful, eternal being deserving of the most amazing things this Universe has to offer, and then take inspired action toward manifesting that life.

Meditate.

I can't even count how many times I've heard people say they are looking for a way to calm down, be less anxious, a way to sleep, and a way to shut down their brain. I suggest meditation and almost immediately hear, "I don't have time for meditation," or "I don't know how to meditate," or "I can't meditate."

Meditation is nothing more than an act of concentrated focus. There is no wrong way to meditate. It doesn't mean you have to lie down in silence looking for the meaning of life from your "I AM" Presence. Your meditation may be sitting for five or ten minutes free-writing whatever comes to mind. It could be that your best meditation is while you are in motion—running, cycling, boxing, cleaning—whatever clears your head and allows you single-mindedness.

Take an attitude of gratitude.

Your beliefs aren't going to shape your children. Your actions are. So, walk your talk, practice what you believe, and your children will practice the same. Raising entitled kids isn't in the best interest of anyone. Be grateful. Show your children how to be grateful.

Be grateful for the situations in your life that have been positive and for those that have been trying which have forced you to grow beyond where you ever thought you would be. You've survived every challenge in your life to this point. You are amazingly strong!

Think positive.

Look for the best in people and situations. Just for today, don't take things personally. Don't assign negative intent to the unintentional actions of others. That driver who just cut you off may be thinking about a sick friend. Your friend who never texted you back about coffee tonight may have just found out their child is being bullied. The person who didn't hold the door for you at Starbucks may have just found out that their spouse is cheating. Everyone has their own issues to deal with. Sometimes those issues cause internal struggle that we as outsiders know nothing about. Their actions may look deliberate or rude, but you can never truly know. Let today be the day you look for the good in everyone and see how it changes your mood, attitude, and thought processes.

Get grounded again.

No, I'm not talking about putting yourself in timeout in your room or taking away a privilege. I'm talking about actively balancing out your energetic body with your physical body. Ever notice how you can feel disconnected and tired, like you are floating, maybe a little flighty? These are all signs that you need to bring yourself back down to Earth. Have a snack, preferably a vegetable or fruit. If possible, try a salt bath. No time for a bath today? Try a quick salt scrub in the shower.

Breathe.

You already did this, but it's important and worth a tenth or twentieth mention. Actually take time to notice your breathing. Do you remember to breathe? Do you hold your breath and not know it? Practicing mindful breathing will actually give you energy and calm every muscle in your body simultaneously . . . and the best part is you can do this anywhere without people thinking you're weird. Try it. Just feel your chest expand and contract as you read these words . . . .

Honor your body and your soul.

Take a rest when needed. Plowing through isn't always what is in your highest good. Being kind, especially with yourself, is always a good idea.

Play calming nature sounds, including water and even meditation music for baby and older ones, alike. It will calm all of you.

Mantras and affirmations.

Find one that works for you. I have given you quite a few to try throughout this book, but ultimately, you have to find the one that works best for you. When I first started using a mantra, mine was "I AM Strong and Resilient." I wrote it on an *Office Space* sticky pad that said "*Work Sucks*" in the background and stuck it to the fridge in my apartment. Each morning, I got a giggle and an affirmation. Today, my mantra is ever-changing but is more like "I AM calm and rested." Try a few . . . you will know when you've found the one that works for you.

Personally, I love the mantra/chant, "Om Namah Shivaya" which means "I bow to Shiva." Shiva is the name given to the consciousness that dwells in us all. Shiva refers to the name of your true identity—your inner self. It essentially means that you love yourself for all good that you contain within your being.

Think Om. Despite its Hindu origin, it has a meaning we can all identify with. By chanting or simply saying the word Om, it is thought that we create within ourselves a vibration that attunes compassion with the universal vibration—and we start thinking limitlessly. If you have ever practiced yoga, you might recognize this as the way each session begins or ends. I find it revitalizing, yet soothing.

Clean it up.

Clearing your space can help to clear your mind. Whenever I notice my mind getting clogged with too many thoughts, too much anxiety, too much stuff, I start clearing out a drawer in my kitchen, or I clean out my kids' drawers or my closet. This small cleansing somehow helps to cleanse the chaos in my mind, too.

Disconnect.

Sometimes we focus on other people too much and can actually begin to take on their issues. We connect with them too much. If you are feeling particularly drained and can't understand why, take a moment and simply ask, "Does this belong to me?" If you feel it doesn't, then set your intention to release it. If it does, then breathe through it.

Make room for more of the good stuff.

When all else fails, sometimes you just need to break down and have a good ole' "cry–fest." Holding it all together and holding it in ALL the time is emotionally exhausting and can many times lead to "mommy (daddy, grandma, grandpa, caretaker) needing a moment." These moments are healthy. They are cathartic. Cleanse those uninvited emotions away so you can make room for more of the good stuff.

Beyond Belief.

I have found through my children that they look at all human beings as they are one. They don't see color, race, or religion. They identify with each and every person they encounter in some way, shape, or form. Through this, I've found myself parenting beyond belief, religious belief, that is. No matter what religious affiliation you have chosen, look for the spirituality in all beings. I was brought up in one religion but have found many truths in all religions. Humans are an intricate web of energy. We are all connected to one another—to Earth. Let's live together in peace and balance.

It's all good.

Every relationship you have is perfect in what it is meant to teach you. Every person in your life, regardless of whether they bring happiness or sadness is perfectly aligned with the lessons you intended to learn in this lifetime. Every person you have ever met is evolving and teaching you lessons that you need to learn in this lifetime. In my life, I know that as long as I keep listening and learning those lessons that the hard moments are teaching me, I am on the right path, my divine path. And the same goes for you . . .

Remember, your children will follow your example, not your advice, so act wisely and deliberately in everything you do.

Exercises:

1. Create a gratitude log. Write daily in it all the things that happened today that you are grateful for. Little, big, seemingly insignificant to others but big for you. Write it all down. When you're feeling low, read it.

2. Notice the people in your life who are happy for your happiness and sad for your sadness. They are the ones who deserve a special place in your heart. Begin today to bring more people like this into your life. Commit by becoming this person for someone you care deeply for. Maybe even start by becoming this person for yourself.

3. Choose one area of your personal space and clean it out. Choose a drawer, closet, cabinet, and clean it out. Declutter the space and watch how cleansing your space also helps to cleanse your mind.

The Zen Parent Guide

Affirmations

My path is one of ease and grace, and I will arrive exactly where I need to be in divine timing.

Everything is always working out for me.

Life is not happening to me. Life is responding to me. Everything I put out is exactly what comes back.

I am a magnet of gratitude.

~ ~ ~

To The Reader

I am Grateful for You.

Thank you for spending your precious time with me. Check back for more tips on finding and maintaining zen as my kids grow older and challenge my peace in different stages of their lives. This book is a collection of my thoughts and experiences, coupled with exercises and affirmations that I've found to be helpful over the years. Please feel free to disregard what you don't like. Take what you like and leave the rest. Namaste.

www.ingramcontent.com/pod-product-compliance
Lightning Source LLC
Chambersburg PA
CBHW071759080526
44588CB00013B/2299